The Fierce 44

Black Americans Who Shook Up the World

Preface by
Kevin Merida

Edited by
Stephen Reiss

Foreword by
Henry Louis
Gates, Jr.

Written by the Staff of The Undefeated
Portraits by Robert Ball

Houghton Mifflin Harcourt
Boston New York

hmhbooks.com

The illustrations in this book were created digitally in Adobe Illustrator.
The text type was set in Bembo.
The display type was set in National.

Designed by Nina Simoneaux

Library of Congress Cataloging-in-Publication Data
Names: Reiss, Stephen, 1957– editor. | Ball, Robert, 1973– illustrator. | The Undefeated (Website) issuing body.
Title: The fierce 44 : black Americans who shook up the world / written by the staff of The Undefeated ; illustrated by Robert Ball ; edited by Stephen Reiss.
Other titles: Fierce forty-four | Black Americans who shook up the world
Description: Boston : Houghton Mifflin Harcourt, [2020] | Includes bibliographical references and index. | Audience: Grades 4–6. | Audience: Ages 10–12.
Identifiers: LCCN 2019006109 (print) | LCCN 2019020583 (ebook) | ISBN 9780358157236 (E-book) | ISBN 9781328940629 (paper over board : alk. paper)
Subjects: LCSH: African Americans—Biography—Juvenile literature.
Classification: LCC E185.96 (ebook) | LCC E185.96 .F54 2020 (print) | DDC 920.0092/96073—dc23
LC record available at https://lccn.loc.gov/2019006109

Manufactured in China
SCP 10 9 8 7 6 5 4 3 2 1
4500776967

Preface

This is a list of the Fierce 44, a collection of dreamers and doers, noisy geniuses and quiet innovators, record breakers and symbols of pride and aspiration.

The group includes a dashing lawyer who redefined fearlessness and broke Jim Crow's back; the most gravity-defying, emulated athlete the world has ever produced; and a brilliant folklorist of spirited independence who was a proudly "outrageous woman."

This is not a list of the Greatest Black Americans of All Time or the Most Influential Blacks in History. Or even the Dopest Brothers and Sisters Who Matter Most This Week. It is a list—fervently debated among the staff of The Undefeated, a list chiseled and refined—of forty-four blacks who shook up the world, or at least their corner of it. We recognize that this is not a complete list of jaw-dropping black achievers; we know that such a list would never run out of names. Why limit ours to forty-four? It's an homage to the forty-fourth president of the United States and the first African American to hold this position, whose own stunning accomplishment was something a lot of us—not to mention our mothers and grandfathers and great-grandmothers—never thought we'd see in our lifetime.

So from Frederick Douglass to Oprah Winfrey to Barack Obama, we hope this collection inspires you to learn more about the incredible contributions black Americans have made to our country.

Kevin Merida
Editor in Chief
The Undefeated, ESPN

Foreword

On the Sunday before his inauguration as the forty-fourth president of the United States in 2009, Barack H. Obama summoned history in an address he delivered at the Lincoln Memorial in Washington, DC.

Abraham Lincoln, enthroned inside the memorial, was among the forty-three American presidents who preceded Obama, but that wasn't the only history behind him. On the eve of his swearing-in as the first black president, Obama was standing on a far firmer foundation: the history of the African American people. The pioneering black historian Carter G. Woodson once wrote that "the accounts of the successful strivings of Negroes for enlightenment under most adverse circumstances read like beautiful romances of a people in an heroic age." Those strivings were interwoven with every president who came before Obama, pushing the country to live up to the ideals of freedom and equal human rights that it had articulated at its founding, even as it retreated from them during both the long age of enslavement and the long retreat from Reconstruction after the Civil War that marked the nadir of race relations in the United States.

Today, we need those "beautiful romances" more than ever. The pages that follow in this gorgeously rendered volume, *The Fierce 44,* fill that need. The artwork by Robert Ball is both mesmerizing and elevating, while the snapshot biographies of the undefeated inside offer exemplary truths and models of action that will be a source of comfort, enlightenment, and courage to every reader. Although this is anything but a comprehensive list of the great heroes of our tradition, it serves up a rousing glimpse of a people who paved the way for our moment of reckoning. I have no doubt you will be as inspired studying their lives as I have been.

Henry Louis Gates, Jr.
Cambridge, MA

The Fierce 44

Because
he gave a
voice to the
voiceless

1

Robert Abbott

FOUNDER OF THE *CHICAGO DEFENDER* • 1870–1940

In 1905, Robert Abbott started the *Chicago Defender,* one of the most important black newspapers in history, with just twenty-five cents (the equivalent of about seven dollars today). What began as a weekly four-page pamphlet distributed in the city's black neighborhoods quickly grew into a national publication with a readership of more than half a million.

The success of the *Defender* made Abbott, the son of former slaves, into one of the nation's most prominent black millionaires and paved the way for other successful black publishers.

At the *Defender,* Abbott encouraged the Great Migration, in which six million African Americans fled the poverty and racially motivated violence of the South for new lives in the West, Northeast, and Midwest. Many of them settled in Chicago, where manufacturing jobs were opening up as World War I approached.

Abbott was a natural hustler, which helped his reputation and the paper's circulation. When the *Defender* was initially banned by white authorities in the South because it encouraged African Americans to abandon the area and head north, Abbott, who was born in Georgia, used a network of black railroad porters to surreptitiously distribute the paper in southern states. His legacy lives on today in black publications such as *Essence* and *Black Enterprise.*

2

Alvin Ailey

FOUNDER OF ALVIN AILEY AMERICAN DANCE THEATER

1931–89

Born into poverty in Texas, choreographer Alvin Ailey drew on his knowledge of close-knit black churches, rural juke joints, fiery protest songs, his lonely childhood, and his adult life as a closeted gay man to fuel his passion for dance.

The modern-dance pioneer and civil rights artist-as-activist created pieces that have become as important to the definition of American art as tap dance, jazz, and hip-hop. His desire to have classically trained black dancers move to the music of Duke Ellington, gospel, blues, and Latin and African pop was revolutionary.

Ailey explored issues of social justice, racism, and spirituality in the African American experience through his art. After a few years of dancing on Broadway, he started his own company in 1958, at the height of the civil rights movement. By 1965, Ailey had stopped performing as a dancer to concentrate on his company and choreographing dances for other performers. He created seventy-nine ballets over the course of his career.

Revelations, which premiered in 1960, is Ailey's most celebrated work. The up-from-slavery dance narrative finds beauty in the midst of tragedy and pain, celebrates black folks' resilience and humanity, and allows hope to overcome tribulation.

Even after Ailey's death from an AIDS-related illness in 1989, the company and school have continued to be the premier spot for emerging black choreographers. The Alvin Ailey American Dance Theater is still one of the most popular dance companies touring internationally and has performed in dozens of countries on six of the seven continents.

Because he brought
the beauty of
black bodies
to the fight
for justice

Because
he was the
greatest,
just like
he said
he was

3

Muhammad Ali

BOXER, ACTIVIST • 1942–2016

Muhammad Ali, who loudly proclaimed himself both pretty and the greatest boxer of all time, set the standard for social activism by athletes.

He was named Cassius Clay when he was born in Louisville, Kentucky, and he started boxing at the age of twelve after someone stole his bike. At eighteen, Clay had won an Olympic gold medal. A short four years later, he beat the heavily favored Sonny Liston to become the world heavyweight champion.

The next day, Clay showed the world that he was more than a great boxer, announcing that he was joining the Nation of Islam and getting rid of his "slave name." He would now be known as Muhammad Ali.

At the time, black athletes were expected to be "credits to the race" by being modest and dignified and staying quiet about issues affecting the country. Ali rejected all of that. He was nicknamed the Louisville Lip, mocking opponents and often forecasting his victory in rhyme. He became a Muslim in a predominantly Christian country. And at a time when fighting for civil rights meant pushing for integration, Ali joined a religious group that preached racial separation.

Ali also questioned America's participation in the Vietnam War and refused to be drafted into the Army. He was stripped of his boxing titles and put on trial for evading the draft. Ali eventually won his case after appealing it all the way to the Supreme Court. But for more than three years, no one would pay him to fight.

After his trial, Ali went on to win the world heavyweight title for an unprecedented third time in a bout against undefeated heavyweight champion George Foreman in the "Rumble in the Jungle" in Kinshasa, Zaire. Ali, at age thirty-two, was the underdog, but with an eighth-round knockout, he reclaimed the title that had been taken from him years earlier because of his opposition to the war.

A lifelong social activist and philanthropist, Ali received many honors for his humanitarian work, including the Presidential Medal of Freedom.

4

Richard Allen

FOUNDER OF THE AFRICAN METHODIST EPISCOPAL (AME) CHURCH

1760–1831

Born into slavery in 1760 in Philadelphia, "Negro Richard" struck a deal in 1780 to buy his freedom and that of his brother a few years later. Richard Allen (the name he chose as a freedman) discovered religion after hearing a Methodist preacher at a secret gathering of slaves in Delaware.

But white Methodists didn't want to pray with blacks. So Allen, his wife, Sarah, and others started the Bethel AME Church on July 29, 1794, in a converted blacksmith shop in Philadelphia. Allen was the church's pastor. It was the beginnings of the country's first independent black denomination, which now has more than six thousand churches with about three million members.

Recognizing that former slaves and freedmen needed education, Allen opened a day school for black children and a night school for adults, as well as created church groups to care for the poor. Many of his sermons and published articles attacked slavery and criticized groups that wanted to send blacks back to Africa. Both Allen's family home and Bethel AME were stops on the Underground Railroad, which gave shelter and aid to slaves escaping from Southern border states.

Because
God doesn't
segregate, but
humans do

Because
she rose to
greatness
despite
cruel
hardships

5

Maya Angelou

WRITER, ACTIVIST • 1928–2014

Maya Angelou lived a life just as remarkable as the poetry and prose she crafted.

She experienced a traumatic childhood marked by sexual abuse and violence and at one point stopped speaking for five years. During this time, she memorized poetry, rearranging cadences and reciting Shakespearean sonnets in her head.

With the help of a teacher, Angelou was able to speak again. She used literature to help her recover from trauma, but she got pregnant at sixteen. She found work as San Francisco's first African American female cable car conductor and took many different jobs to support her family.

Later, she joined the Harlem Writers Guild and, with help from fellow author James Baldwin, went on to write *I Know Why the Caged Bird Sings*—the first in what would become a seven-volume best-selling autobiographical series. Nearly a decade later, Angelou finished *And Still I Rise,* a poetry collection that remains one of her most important works. Her writing earned her many awards, including three Grammys and the Presidential Medal of Freedom.

Angelou was also a fearless civil rights activist, serving as a coordinator for Martin Luther King Jr.'s Southern Christian Leadership Conference (SCLC) and working with Malcolm X to establish the Organization of Afro-American Unity.

Life tried hard to break Angelou, but in the face of it all, she rose.

6

Ella Baker

CIVIL RIGHTS ACTIVIST • 1903–86

Ella Baker's grandmother, a former slave, used to tell her a story about being threatened with a whipping for refusing to marry a man whom her owner's wife had selected for her. That story helped fuel Baker's lifelong quest for justice for her people. She became one of the most important behind-the-scenes organizers in the civil rights movement.

In the 1940s, Baker worked at the National Association for the Advancement of Colored People (NAACP), helping to convince black people that the United States could and should exist "without discrimination based on race." In 1957, she moved to Atlanta to help Martin Luther King Jr. form the SCLC, organizing protests and running a voter registration campaign called the Crusade for Citizenship. But Baker grew frustrated with the leadership style of the men at the top of the organization who didn't know how to deal with a strong woman.

Inspired by four college students who refused to leave a lunch counter at Woolworth's in Greensboro, North Carolina, after they were denied service, Baker helped create the Student Nonviolent Coordinating Committee, or SNCC. Pronounced "Snick," the group emphasized voting rights for African Americans and helped organize the Freedom Rides, in which black and white students tried to desegregate bus terminals in the South.

Baker's nickname was "Fundi," which is Swahili for a person who teaches a craft to the next generation. Baker viewed young people as one of the strongest and most important aspects of the civil rights movement. As long as they had the audacity to dream of a better, equal, and brighter tomorrow, and were willing to work for it through peaceful protest, a fairer society awaited them.

Because
she didn't
let gender
keep her
from
defending
her race

Because he embraced the responsibility to be a voice of his nation

7

James Baldwin

NOVELIST, PLAYWRIGHT • 1924–87

James Baldwin knew it was his job to reveal the truth: The truth about his race. The truth about his country. The ugly truths of racism, poverty, and inequality that plague the United States even now.

He confronted American racism with fearless honesty, and he did it with style. His brilliant prose combined his own experience with the best and worst of the black life around him: the joy, the blues, the sermons, the spirituals, and the bitter sting of discrimination.

Baldwin grew up in Harlem, where his writing talent was recognized at an early age. He moved to Europe when he was twenty-four after becoming discouraged by the racism in the United States. His first novel, *Go Tell It on the Mountain,* illuminated the struggle of poor inner-city residents. His collection of essays called *The Fire Next Time* explosively represented black identity just as the country was coming to terms with how much white supremacy helped shape our history. In his second novel, *Giovanni's Room,* Baldwin wrote about homosexuality—exploring sexual identity without ever mentioning race.

As an impoverished black gay man, Baldwin was asked if he felt he'd had bad luck. In fact, he said, he believed he'd hit the jackpot. His identity helped to create his work. And his writing represented every individual whose access to American civil liberties was hampered by race, gender, sexuality, or poverty.

Baldwin unapologetically asked the nation to see its true self through the beauty of its most marginalized people.

8

Jean-Michel Basquiat

ARTIST • 1960–88

Eight short years: that's how long it took Jean-Michel Basquiat to secure his legacy as a great artist. He died at the age of twenty-seven from a drug overdose, leaving behind paintings, drawings, and notebooks, many of which explored American punk and hip-hop, the urban plight of African Americans, jazz, and the nature of fame during the 1980s.

Born to a Haitian father and Puerto Rican mother, Basquiat dropped out of high school and started doing graffiti art on New York City's Lower East Side. He was handsome, fashionable, and famously eccentric.

The drawing in Basquiat's best-known pieces may look primitive, but the images are complex and sophisticated. While his worldview was undeniably black, urban, and hypermasculine, his bold technique featuring splashes of paint was influenced by modern abstract masters Jackson Pollock and Cy Twombly. But there is also a connection to early twentieth-century African American greats such as Romare Bearden and Jacob Lawrence.

As influential as Basquiat is, most of his work is privately owned and few museums have any of his best-known pieces. His paintings attract stratospheric prices when they are put up for auction. In 2017, Basquiat's 1982 *Untitled* painting sold for $110.5 million, a record high for any American painter, making him the most successful African American painter in history. Celebrities collect his work, and an entire generation of hip-hop artists—Kanye West, Jay-Z, Lil Wayne, Killer Mike, Rick Ross, and J. Cole—have name-checked Basquiat. In other words, legendary dopeness and enigmatic brilliance never go out of style.

Because
legendary
dopeness
never goes
out of style

Because she left
us a legacy of
love, hope,
and dignity

9

Mary McLeod Bethune

CIVIL RIGHTS ACTIVIST, EDUCATOR • 1875–1955

Though she was able-bodied, Mary McLeod Bethune carried a cane because she said it gave her "swank."

An educator, civil rights leader, and advisor to four U.S. presidents, the "First Lady of the Struggle" has been synonymous with black uplift since the early twentieth century. She turned her faith, her passion for racial progress, and her organizational and fundraising savvy into the enduring legacies of Bethune-Cookman University and the National Council of Negro Women.

Bethune, the fifteenth of seventeen children, her parents former slaves, grew up in rural South Carolina and started working in the fields as a young girl. She hoped to become a missionary in Africa after attending seminaries in North Carolina and Illinois but was told black missionaries were unwelcome. So she turned to educating her people at home, founding the Daytona Literary and Industrial Training School for Negro Girls in 1904 with $1.50 and a handful of students. The school later merged with Cookman Institute, a school for African American boys. Bethune served as president, one of the few female college presidents in the nation at the time, and also became president of the National Association of Colored Women. A decade later, Bethune founded the influential National Council of Negro Women.

Bethune helped organize black advisors to serve on the Federal Council of Negro Affairs, the storied "Black Cabinet," under President Franklin D. Roosevelt. First Lady Eleanor Roosevelt considered Bethune one of her closest friends.

Bethune worked to end poll taxes and lynching. She organized protests against businesses that refused to hire African Americans. Her entire life, she organized, she wrote, she lectured, and she inspired.

10

Simone Biles

GYMNAST • 1997–

Simone Arianne Biles, born in Columbus, Ohio, and raised outside of Houston, Texas, was six when an impromptu field trip changed her life. She and her classmates were at a local gymnastics center where a coach noticed that Biles just couldn't stand still and was bouncing all over the mats.

Biles's family signed her up for classes, and her boundless energy, amazing physicality, and acrobatic bravery took flight. Biles, who stands four feet, eight inches tall, began competing internationally in 2013. Later that year, she became only the seventh American and the first African American to win the world all-around gymnastics title.

But she was just getting started.

Biles is the first woman to win three consecutive world all-around titles, and in the 2016 Rio de Janeiro Olympics she won gold medals in the vault, floor exercise, individual all-around, and team all-around competition. She invented two moves, one in the floor exercise and another in the vault, that are named after her. Her routines are so difficult that she almost fell off the balance beam and still won a bronze medal in Rio.

Biles's accomplishments are even more remarkable because of her childhood. When her birth mother was unable to care for her, Biles and her siblings spent years in foster care before her grandfather and his wife adopted her and her little sister, Adria. Biles now advocates on behalf of foster children and says being part of a family helped her feel like she mattered. So did finding her passion for gymnastics.

Her twisting, high-flying precision moves, including ones that didn't exist before she made them up, have led many gymnastics judges and fans to consider her the best athlete in the history of the sport.

Because
the most
dominant
gymnast
ever is still
inventing
new moves

Because before "Yes We Can" there was "Unbought and Unbossed"

11

Shirley Chisholm

POLITICIAN • 1924–2005

Before President Barack Obama's "Yes We Can" slogan, there was Shirley Chisholm's motto, "Unbought and Unbossed."

In 1972, thirty-six years before Obama was elected the first black president, Chisholm was the first black candidate for a major party's nomination for president. That campaign made her a pathbreaker for women, too: she was the first woman to run for the Democratic Party's presidential nomination, forty-four years before Hillary Clinton became the first woman to win a major party's nomination for president.

Being the first wasn't anything new for Chisholm. In 1968, she became the first black woman elected to Congress, representing New York for seven terms from 1969 to 1983. As both a New York state legislator and a congresswoman, Chisholm fought for the federal government to help people get an education and to help poor people get enough food to eat.

Chisholm noted that she faced more discrimination because of gender than race during her legislative career, while acknowledging the additional struggle that black women encounter because of their color. Every person Chisholm hired for her congressional office was a woman, and half of them were black.

Chisholm wanted women, African Americans, and the poor to get a seat at the table. And if there wasn't an empty chair, she advised bringing your own.

12

Benjamin O. Davis Sr.

U.S. ARMY GENERAL • 1880–1970

Benjamin Oliver Davis Sr. began his military career in the Spanish-American War as a volunteer in the infantry. (It is thought he may have even lied about his age so he could enlist without his parents' permission.) He liked the discipline and order, so a few months after he was discharged, he reenlisted and stayed in the military for the rest of his career. Four decades later, as the United States prepared to enter World War II, Davis became the first African American general in the Army.

America's military was segregated for most of Davis's career, and black soldiers had limited options for promotion. His duty assignments were designed to avoid putting him in command of white troops or officers. Davis led troops in Liberia and the Philippines, where he served with the famed all-black Buffalo Soldiers. He was assigned as a professor of military science and tactics at both Wilberforce University in Ohio and Tuskegee Institute in Alabama. He rose slowly through the ranks, becoming the first black colonel in the Army in 1930.

In 1940, Davis was promoted to brigadier general by President Franklin D. Roosevelt. During World War II, Davis headed a special unit charged with safeguarding the status and morale of black soldiers in the Army, and he served in Europe as a special advisor on race relations.

Davis retired in 1948 after fifty years of service. Six days later, President Harry S. Truman ordered the end of discriminatory practices in the armed forces.

Davis's determined and disciplined rise in the Army paved the way for black men and women—including his son, Benjamin O. Davis Jr., who in 1954 became the second African American general in the U.S. military and the first in the Air Force.

Because he led the fight against enemies both foreign and domestic

Because his voice rose from slavery to challenge the denial of black humanity

13

Frederick Douglass

ABOLITIONIST, AUTHOR • 1818–95

Born on a Maryland farm in 1818, Frederick Douglass was the son of a slave mother and a white father who may have been his owner. When Douglass was eight, he was sent to Baltimore to work for a ship carpenter. The carpenter's wife started to teach him to read, and Douglass recognized there was a connection between knowledge and freedom. At fifteen, Douglass was sent to a different farm to work for a brutal man with a reputation as a "slave breaker." Douglass hated the man and his time on the farm and tried to escape.

Eventually, Douglass was sent back to Baltimore where he worked as a slave in a shipyard. When he turned twenty, he met a free black woman who helped him escape. She bought him a train ticket to New York, and, disguised as a sailor, he was on his way to freedom.

Once he was in the North, Douglass started to talk to antislavery groups about his personal experience. He was a dynamic speaker who knew how to hold an audience. He was tall and graceful and had a voice that made you pay attention to what he had to say.

Some people doubted that such a good speaker could have been a slave. So in 1845, Douglass wrote an autobiography, *Narrative of the Life of Frederick Douglass,* with all the details of his upbringing. A vivid portrayal of physical brutality, mental torture, and the separation of family members, the memoir brought the horrors of slavery into the light and became the most influential personal story of slavery in U.S. history. Besides fighting for abolition, Douglass was also an outspoken supporter for women's rights and continued to push for equality all his life.

14

Charles Drew

PHYSICIAN • 1904–50

As a young man, Charles Drew was an exceptional athlete, starring in football, baseball, basketball, and track and field at Dunbar High School in Washington, DC. He was an All-American halfback and captain of the track team at Amherst College in Massachusetts. Because he couldn't afford medical school in the United States, Drew attended McGill University in Montreal but later moved back to the United States to teach at Howard University's medical school.

Drew went on to do research at Columbia University in New York, becoming the first African American to get a medical doctorate at the prestigious school. He became the world's leading authority on blood transfusions and storage. His research established procedures for how blood should be collected and refrigerated and how blood donors should be recruited and screened, as well as training methods for people who would collect and test blood. His research on plasma, the liquid portion of blood without cells, made it possible for blood to be "banked" for long periods of time.

Drew's work was especially important as the United States prepared for World War II. As medical director of the American Red Cross National Blood Donor Service, Drew led the collection of tens of thousands of pints of blood for U.S. troops. Some historians say Drew's work may have saved the world from Nazism, since battlefield blood storage and transfusions didn't exist before then.

When the U.S. military ruled that the blood of African Americans would be segregated and not used on white troops, even though blood has no racial characteristics, Drew was outraged and resigned from the Red Cross. He returned to Washington, DC, as a professor at Howard University and head of surgery at Freedmen's Hospital, where he trained many black physicians. Drew continued to work as a physician until his untimely death in a car crash.

Because he was a medical pioneer who saved millions of lives

Because he explained the conflicted nature of being African American

15

W. E. B. Du Bois

SOCIOLOGIST, WRITER, ACTIVIST • 1868–1963

William Edward Burghardt Du Bois, the first African American to receive a PhD from Harvard University, was a brilliant scholar who changed how black people saw their place in the world. But he was also a political activist who helped start the NAACP, crusaded against lynching, and tried to unite black people across the world.

His most famous book, *The Souls of Black Folk,* was published in 1903 and introduced the idea of "double consciousness," in which blacks always have to think about how white people see them. Du Bois rejected the arguments of Booker T. Washington, the most influential black leader of the time, who asked blacks to accept discrimination while trying to prove they were worthy of equal treatment through hard work. Instead, Du Bois believed, blacks should actively fight discrimination and racism.

Du Bois acted on his beliefs. He helped start the NAACP and was the founder and first editor of its crusading magazine, *The Crisis.* He criticized President Woodrow Wilson for resegregating the federal government and continually spoke up for social justice. Du Bois ran for the U.S. Senate in New York, representing the American Labor Party, and became chair of the Peace Information Center, which sought to ban nuclear weapons around the world. At one point, Du Bois was arrested and charged with being an agent of the Soviet Union. He was found not guilty and later moved to Ghana, where he stayed until the end of his life.

16

Duke Ellington

COMPOSER, BANDLEADER • 1899–1974

Edward "Duke" Ellington started playing piano as a seven-year-old, and by the time he was seventeen, he was working as a professional musician. A few years later, he moved to New York City and was soon a regular at the famous Cotton Club in Harlem, launching a career as one of the greatest American musicians of all time.

Just as soul music and Motown provided the soundtrack for the 1960s civil rights movement, big band swing music furnished the score for the Harlem Renaissance of the 1920s. While many famous bandleaders were playing then, including Count Basie and Benny Goodman, Ellington was the best.

A pianist and an orchestra leader, music seemed to pour from Ellington. He wrote more than one thousand tunes, many of which are considered classics, including "Don't Get Around Much Anymore," and "Satin Doll." His original songs rank among the first examples of crossover pop. They captured the essence of the black experience, but were also irresistible to white audiences.

Unlike other bandleaders, who wanted their musicians to meld their sounds together, Ellington was famous for writing music to highlight individual artists. He liked to feature people with unique styles and was constantly rewriting even his biggest hits.

Ellington received many honors, including eleven Grammy Awards, thirteen Grammy Hall of Fame nods, the Presidential Medal of Freedom, and a Pulitzer Prize special citation, and was inducted into the Songwriters Hall of Fame. But Sir Duke's legacy is bigger than any award. Whenever "swing" or "big band music" is mentioned, Ellington's name leaps to mind as he is the embodiment of jazz.

Because
he is the
embodiment
of jazz

Because
the Queen
of Soul deserves
respect

17

Aretha Franklin

SINGER-SONGWRITER • 1942–2018

In 1967, Aretha Franklin, the daughter of popular Detroit Baptist minister C. L. Franklin, scored a number one hit with her remake of Otis Redding's "Respect." The song became part of the soundtrack of the civil rights movement as well as an anthem for the women's movement as women demanded to be taken as seriously as men.

But Franklin was bigger than one track. She had started out as a teenager singing gospel music. Soon, she branched out and, over the years, moved easily from jazz to rhythm and blues to pop. At the Grammy Awards in 1998, she stepped in at the last minute for a sick opera star and dazzled the audience with her performance. But Franklin always brought her roots in gospel to her songs, which is why she was nicknamed the Queen of Soul.

Franklin was a big supporter of the civil rights movement, one time going on tour with other artists to help raise money for the cause. She sang at the memorial service for Martin Luther King Jr., who was a friend of her father's. She also sang at the inauguration of the first black president, Barack Obama.

In 1987, Franklin became the first female performer inducted into the Rock & Roll Hall of Fame. Over her six-decade career, she had more than one hundred singles on the *Billboard* charts, and seventeen of them were top-ten singles. She won eighteen Grammys and sold more than seventy-five million albums.

Franklin was a musician's musician: she could bang it out on the piano and sang opera as effortlessly as gospel. Few can match her four-octave range or sustain a note or a song quite the way Franklin did. All hail the Queen.

18

Jimi Hendrix

MUSICIAN, SINGER-SONGWRITER • 1942–70

Jimi Hendrix couldn't read or write music. But *Rolling Stone* magazine named him the greatest guitar player ever. The Rock & Roll Hall of Fame went even further, calling him "the most gifted instrumentalist of all time."

Hendrix left his home in Seattle in 1961 to become a paratrooper in the Army. After suffering an injury from a parachute jump, he left the military and started working as a backup musician for some of the best rhythm and blues acts of the time.

Soon, Hendrix began his short career as a headliner, radically changing how the electric guitar was played and combining rock with blues and jazz. He was popular with white audiences even while playing music built on the black experience.

What made Hendrix so great? His live performances could be messy and his guitar tone ear-piercing. But it was these eccentricities that made him unique. For Hendrix, music wasn't about a note-perfect performance but a search for truth. He was a nonconformist and part of a generation that was proud to be antiestablishment.

Hendrix died at only twenty-seven after an overdose, but by then he had thoroughly changed how people thought about music. Hendrix's talent is probably best demonstrated by his performance of "The Star-Spangled Banner" at the famous Woodstock music festival in 1969, in which he used his guitar to condemn the war in Vietnam by evoking the sounds of artillery explosions and air-raid sirens.

Many guitarists have challenged Hendrix's position at the top, yet none have matched his genius. In the world of electric guitar, there are two ages: the monochromatic era Before Hendrix and the limitless, kaleidoscopic period After Hendrix.

Because the greatest guitar player ever changed all of music

Because she inspired
pride in southern
black culture

19

Zora Neale Hurston

NOVELIST, WRITER • 1891–1960

Zora Neale Hurston is now recognized as one of the South's most famous and eloquent writers, but it took a long time for her talent to be recognized.

She grew up in Eatonville, Florida, the first all-black incorporated town in the country, where her father was one of the first mayors. Her mother, a Sunday school teacher who encouraged her children to be ambitious, died when Hurston was only thirteen. She didn't get along with her stepmother and eventually joined a group of traveling performers as a maid.

She finally finished high school in her twenties before going on to get degrees from Howard University in Washington, DC, and Barnard College in New York City, where she studied anthropology.

In New York, Hurston became a central figure in the Harlem Renaissance of the 1920s and pursued a career as a writer and researcher who studied the folklore of southern blacks. The author of four novels, including the now-celebrated *Their Eyes Were Watching God* (1937), and the autobiography *Dust Tracks on a Road* (1942), she also wrote short stories, essays, and plays. Unlike other writers, Hurston focused on the experience of black women and wrote the way black people in the South actually spoke.

Hurston never made much money from her writing. When she died, her neighbors in Fort Pierce, Florida, couldn't afford a headstone, so they buried her in an unmarked grave. Alice Walker (who later wrote *The Color Purple*) found her grave in 1972 and paid for a marker. Now everyone recognizes Hurston as an important author who told the story of country folk.

20

Jesse Jackson

CIVIL RIGHTS ACTIVIST, POLITICIAN • 1941–

Jesse Jackson's are the biggest shoulders that Barack Obama stands on. Jackson laid the foundation for electing a black president, one of the signature achievements of the twenty-first century.

The groundwork began with Jackson's decision to run for president himself in 1984, widely seen then as more symbolic than practical. Black leaders had discussed for years what it would take to seriously compete for the highest office in the land. After Harold Washington was elected Chicago's first black mayor in 1983 and with concern mounting about the negative impact of Ronald Reagan's presidency on black Americans, some thought it was time. Jackson was one of the greatest political orators in American history. His ability to inspire farmers and factory workers, maids who take the bus, and teenagers growing up in housing projects was unmatched.

In 1984, Jackson ran for president and won five Democratic primaries and caucuses on a tiny budget. With his second presidential campaign in 1988, he established himself as the leader of the progressive wing of the Democratic Party. He won eleven primaries and caucuses and finished as runner-up to Democratic nominee Michael Dukakis.

Before Jackson's campaigns, black campaign workers were largely put in small roles focused on "urban issues." Jackson helped increase black participation in all the jobs in politics. The result was more field operatives, strategists, and fundraisers—and candidates for a wider range of offices—than ever before.

He deserves credit for his civil rights activism in the Deep South and later on Wall Street and in Silicon Valley. But Jackson's most notable achievement was demonstrating that sending an African American to the Oval Office was an attainable dream.

Because
he kept
hope alive
and made
the White
House a
realistic
goal

Because he's
the greatest
man in hip-hop
NY

21

Jay-Z

ARTIST, ENTREPRENEUR • 1969–

Shawn Corey Carter grew up in the Marcy Projects in Brooklyn, New York, where his mother, Gloria Carter, remembers he'd be in the kitchen of their apartment rapping until late at night. He never graduated from high school and initially sold CDs out of his car. He became Jay-Z with his 1996 debut album, *Reasonable Doubt*. Ten years later, MTV named him the greatest rapper of all time.

Famous for his work ethic, Jay-Z has released fourteen *Billboard* number one albums, the most by any solo artist in history. These include many timeless tracks that have defined popular culture, such as 2004's "99 Problems," a look at what it's like to drive while black in America, and 2009's "D.O.A. (Death of Auto-Tune)," which single-handedly undermined a voice-correction tool that was widely used in rap and pop music. Jay-Z was instrumental in taking hip-hop from its origins in house parties to selling out stadium concerts.

As he climbed the charts, Jay-Z also became an influential businessman. He is an owner of Tidal, a streaming music service. He cofounded Roc-A-Fella Records, served as president of Def Jam Recordings, founded entertainment company Roc Nation, and became part-owner of the Brooklyn Nets before giving up his stake in the NBA franchise to found his own sports agency, Roc Nation Sports.

Married to Beyoncé, Jay-Z has lived the American dream of reinvention and second chances.

22

Katherine Johnson

MATHEMATICIAN, PHYSICIST • 1918–

By fourth grade, every American kid has studied the history of this country's space missions, especially the story of astronaut John Glenn, who became the first American to orbit the earth in 1962. But for a long time, one nugget was missing from those histories—the black woman who helped him safely get there and back.

Katherine Johnson was a physicist and mathematician, one of many black women hired by NASA in the early 1950s to work in the Guidance and Navigation Department. She was a math prodigy who graduated from high school at fourteen and earned a double degree in math and French from West Virginia State College at eighteen. *And* she helped to integrate the graduate school at West Virginia University, where she was one of three black students and the only black woman.

At NASA, Johnson was plucked from the pool of women working on math calculations to work with an all-male flight research team. Besides her work on Glenn's famous flight, she helped launch the use of computers at the space agency and helped calculate the orbit for the 1969 Apollo 11 flight to the moon. Johnson coauthored twenty-six scientific papers in her career at NASA.

In 2015, then-president Barack Obama awarded Johnson the Presidential Medal of Freedom for her pioneering work. And the next year, her story was told in grand Hollywood fashion in the movie *Hidden Figures.* Taraji P. Henson played the role of Johnson and brought to life a story that many of us never knew existed.

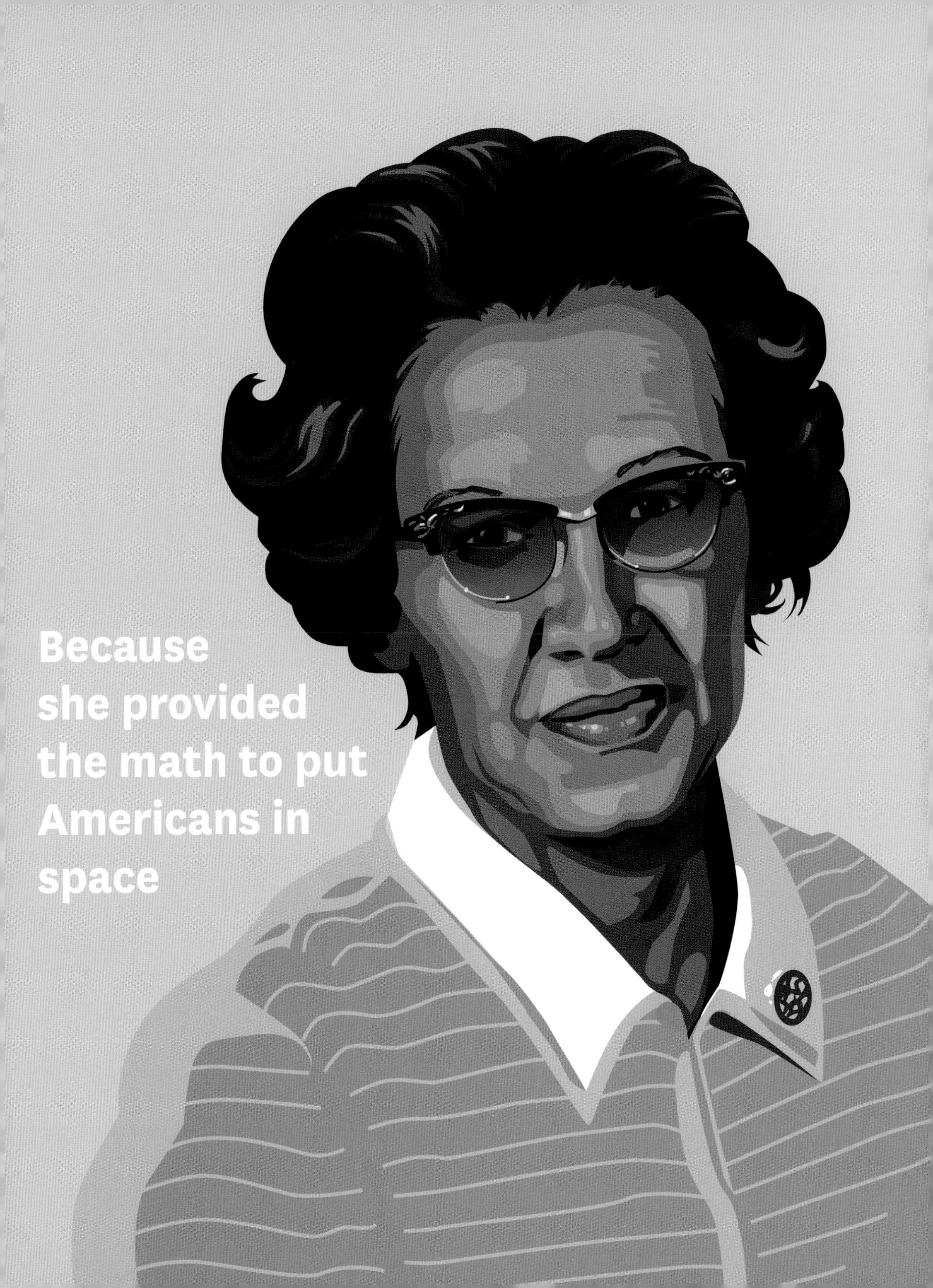
Because
she provided
the math to put
Americans in
space

Because he is producing
the soundtrack
of our lives

23

Quincy Jones

MUSIC PRODUCER, SONGWRITER, ACTIVIST • 1933–

Many words can be used to describe Quincy Jones, but let's start with innovator. Others that work: producer, writer, arranger, composer, and humanitarian. He has had an impact on music and popular culture for six decades, helping make some of the best-selling albums of all time.

Jones is responsible for a number of firsts in music, movies, and television, and has paved the way for other African Americans in the entertainment industry. In 1967, Jones became the first black composer to be nominated for two Academy Awards within the same year. In 1971, he was the first black musical director and conductor for the Oscars show. And in 1995, Jones was the first black person to receive the Jean Hersholt Humanitarian Award from the Academy of Motion Picture Arts and Sciences. Jones has earned seventy-nine Grammy nominations, has collected twenty-seven Grammys, and was honored with a Grammy Legend Award in 1991.

He produced all three of Michael Jackson's iconic albums—*Off the Wall, Bad,* and *Thriller*—the last of which sold more than thirty-three million copies in the United States alone. In 1985, Jones sealed his reputation as a humanitarian by gathering more than three dozen of the biggest names in music in one studio to record the song "We Are the World." The song raised money for famine relief in Africa and is one of the highest-selling singles of all time.

Jones's influence extends across many media. In 1993, he founded *Vibe* magazine, an entertainment publication that gave urban Generation Xers a periodical that reflected themselves. Even now, in his eighties, Jones isn't done. He's been working on a subscription service for vinyl records and collaborating on a new brand of headphones.

24

Michael Jordan

BASKETBALL PLAYER, NBA TEAM OWNER • 1963–

In 1978, Michael Jordan was a sophomore in high school and didn't get picked for the varsity basketball team. That setback helped create a ruthless competitor who went on to become one of the most dominant athletes in any sport.

Jordan accepted a scholarship to the University of North Carolina at Chapel Hill, where he played for three years. He scored the game-winning basket to clinch a national championship in his freshman year and swept all the national player of the year awards in his junior year. In the 1984 NBA draft, the Chicago Bulls selected him third overall.

Jordan is regarded by many as the best player ever to touch a basketball. His six NBA titles in six NBA Finals appearances with six NBA Finals MVP Awards are among the greatest feats ever seen in sports. He's won five league MVPs, ten league scoring titles, an NBA Defensive Player of the Year Award, two NBA Slam Dunk Contest trophies—and the list goes on.

He turned Air Jordan into a billion-dollar brand for shoes, clothing, and accessories. Jordan left basketball at the peak of his playing career to play minor league baseball. When that didn't go well, he announced his return to the NBA with a two-word fax that read, "I'm back," and went on to win three more championships.

After his playing days ended, Jordan became the majority owner of the Charlotte Hornets, the first former player to reach that level. And in 2016, in a rare public statement on social justice, he said he could "no longer stay silent" about the killings of African Americans and targeting of police officers, making a two-million-dollar donation to help address the problem.

Ruthless, relentless, and peerless. That's the Jordan way.

Because he may be the best player ever to touch a basketball

Because he was
the warrior of
nonviolence

25

Martin Luther King Jr.

CIVIL RIGHTS ACTIVIST, BAPTIST MINISTER • 1929–68

In April 1963, Martin Luther King Jr. sat in a jail cell in Birmingham, Alabama. He had been arrested for leading marches and sit-ins to protest racial segregation and was troubled when a group of white ministers criticized the protests.

King responded to them with the famous "Letter from a Birmingham Jail." In this letter, originally written on scraps of paper, he described the racial and economic apartheid facing blacks in the United States. He tried to encourage the people who worried that the fight against segregation would never succeed. And he dismissed those who thought good behavior was more important than justice.

A Baptist minister, King practiced nonviolent protest. But he was committed to radically changing how America treated its black citizens. Later that year, King helped organize the March on Washington, which brought 250,000 protesters to Washington, DC, demanding equality for all Americans. Standing in front of the Lincoln Memorial, King delivered his "I Have a Dream" speech, one of the most famous addresses in American history, in which he talked about his hope that one day whites and blacks could join hands as equals.

King was a man of incredible achievement: He was president of the SCLC, one of the most important groups in the civil rights movement. He helped lead the Montgomery bus boycott, which forced the city to integrate its buses. In 1964, he won the Nobel Peace Prize.

In 1968, King went to Memphis to support a strike by sanitation workers and was shot to death by a sniper. After his assassination, a federal holiday was created in his honor. And like George Washington, Thomas Jefferson, and Abraham Lincoln, there's a monument dedicated to King in Washington.

26

Henrietta Lacks

HeLa CELL LINE • 1920–51

Henrietta Lacks was an accidental pioneer of modern-day medicine. She was thirty-one years old and had five children when she was diagnosed with cervical cancer. Just months before her death, doctors at Johns Hopkins Hospital in Baltimore took pieces of tissue from her cancerous tumor without her consent. Lacks was not a slave, but parts of her cancerous tumor represent the first isolated human cells ever bought and sold.

Her cells, known among scientists as HeLa, were unusual in that they could rapidly reproduce and stay alive long enough to undergo multiple tests. Descendants of Lacks's cells live in laboratories across the world and are worth billions of dollars. They played an important part in developing the polio vaccine, cloning, gene mapping, and in vitro fertilization. The HeLa cell line has been used to develop drugs for treating herpes, leukemia, influenza, and Parkinson's disease. The cells have been influential in the study of cancer, lactose digestion, sexually transmitted diseases, and appendicitis.

While scientists knew her name, for many years her own family did not know how her cells were being used or that billions of dollars had been made because of those experiments. It wasn't until a writer named Rebecca Skloot started a book about Lacks and the HeLa cell line that the public learned what had happened and how little her husband and children knew about her legacy.

Her cells are saving lives today, but no doctor can be proud of how Lacks was treated.

Because she was the subject of a medical experiment that is still saving lives today

Because he sought
to ignite equality
by any means
necessary

27

Malcolm X

CIVIL RIGHTS ACTIVIST, MINISTER • 1925–65

Malcolm X was the American dream, whether America wanted him to be or not. He overcame drug addiction and a life of crime to become one of the country's foremost civil rights leaders and a champion of black pride.

Born Malcolm Little, he converted to Islam while serving a seven-year prison sentence for burglary. He changed his name to Malcolm X because Little was the name imposed on his father's family by white slave masters. Less than two years after his release from prison, he became a minister at Nation of Islam temples in Boston, Philadelphia, and New York.

In 1957, Malcolm X founded the Nation of Islam newspaper *Muhammad Speaks.* For a time in the 1960s, it was the most widely read black newspaper in the United States, and it enabled him to spread his revolutionary message of black pride. Malcolm X's theories became the blueprint for the Black Power movements of the '60s and '70s, and he is also credited with inspiring the idea that "black is beautiful."

Although he'd been known for segregationist views and accepting violence in the quest for equality, Malcolm X took a more diplomatic stance after he left the Nation of Islam in 1964. He began to preach peaceful resistance and the benefits of integration. But that stage of his life was brief because he was assassinated by members of the Nation the following year at the age of thirty-nine.

The Autobiography of Malcolm X, which was published after his death, became an immediate bestseller. It is essential reading for any American.

28

Thurgood Marshall

SUPREME COURT JUSTICE • 1908–93

By the time Thurgood Marshall was nominated to be a Supreme Court justice in 1967, few lawyers in history had argued, and won, more cases before the nation's highest court. Marshall had racked up twenty-nine wins (and just three losses), including his most famous victory, *Brown v. Board of Education,* the 1954 decision that forced public schools to desegregate.

Marshall is arguably the most pivotal figure in the destruction of Jim Crow segregation and the most consequential lawyer of the twentieth century. While other civil rights leaders organized vital sit-ins, marches, and boycotts, Marshall attacked inequality and racism in America's laws. As the NAACP's lead attorney, he traveled the South, filing briefs in local courthouses, representing poor black defendants in criminal cases, and doing battle against racist white juries and judges.

Marshall traveled fifty thousand miles a year, often alone in some of the nation's most dangerous cities and towns. He stayed in the homes of appreciative black folks who took elaborate steps to keep him safe and a step ahead of marauding Klansmen. He managed to maintain his strength amid daily death threats, sipping bourbon and telling stories.

He feared no one—including his colleagues on the Supreme Court, with whom he occasionally clashed during his twenty-four years there—and was a tireless fighter for justice.

It was fitting that Marshall was called Mr. Civil Rights. Across the South, when innocent men were jailed or families were forced to flee from homes destroyed by the Klan, people comforted themselves with two words: "Thurgood's coming."

Because he was
the most feared
black man in
the South

Because she believed everyone has a story to tell

29

Toni Morrison

NOVELIST • 1931–2019

Toni Morrison, the daughter of a welder and a domestic worker, said her parents gave her a love of reading. She grew up to be one of the greatest writers in history and was the first African American to win the Nobel Prize in Literature.

Morrison taught English to college students for several years before moving to New York, where she worked as one of the few black women at the upper levels of a book publishing company. She helped promote the work of black writers and was one of the primary editors of *The Black Book,* a pathbreaking 1974 collection of photos, songs, posters, and drawings that documented the joy and pain of the Africans brought to America and the generations that followed them.

Morrison also wrote her own novels, which told the stories of African American characters, especially women, struggling to find their way in a racist society. Her first novel, *The Bluest Eye,* was about a dark-skinned girl who thought her life would be better if she could have blue eyes.

Her 1977 novel, *Song of Solomon,* became the first work by an African American author in almost forty years to be a featured selection of the Book of the Month Club. Another novel, *Beloved,* won the Pulitzer Prize for Fiction and was turned into a movie starring Oprah Winfrey. It is based on the true story of a runaway slave who, about to be recaptured, kills her infant daughter rather than have her live as a slave. In 2012, Morrison was awarded the Presidential Medal of Freedom by Barack Obama.

30

Barack Obama

44TH PRESIDENT OF THE UNITED STATES • 1961–

Barack Hussein Obama's stride into history has been as confident as it has been unlikely.

He announced his candidacy for president on February 10, 2007, as a first-term U.S. senator who previously had served just seven years in the Illinois Senate. He had little support from established politicians, and many black voters did not even know who he was. But his campaign became a movement. His soaring speeches promising hope and change inspired millions. Less than two years later, a record crowd gathered on the National Mall to witness what was once unthinkable: the inauguration of the first black president of the United States.

It was a singular achievement by a man with a singular history. Obama was born in Hawaii to a Kenyan father and white mother. As a child, he lived in Indonesia before returning to Hawaii to be raised by his white grandparents.

As a teenager, Obama began to discover his black identity largely through basketball. He admired and emulated the loose-limbed swagger of the guys who played the game. He saw black as cool, and he embraced the virtues of blackness while managing to sidestep much of its complicated baggage.

Through two terms as president, Obama oversaw economic growth, rescued the struggling auto industry, and enacted a historic health care reform law. Speaking to the nation in his farewell address, Obama used the slogan that accompanied his history-making rise to the White House: "Yes we can," he said. "Yes we did. Yes we can."

Because he was the president of the United States of America

Because he was the athlete who humiliated Hitler

31

Jesse Owens

TRACK AND FIELD ATHLETE • 1913–80

As a twenty-one-year-old college student, James Cleveland "Jesse" Owens turned in what is probably the greatest day in sports history in less than an hour. Owens started his afternoon at the Big Ten Track and Field Championships in 1935 by tying the world record in the 100-yard dash. Ten minutes later, he set a world record in the long jump. Over the next half hour, he broke world records in the 220-yard dash and the 220-yard low hurdles. Remarkably, he had fallen down some stairs a few days before and badly hurt his back.

The next year, Owens used his speed to beat racism. Heading into the 1936 Olympics in Berlin, Adolf Hitler, the German dictator, claimed that no dark-skinned person could compete with the blond-haired, blue-eyed "Aryan master race."

Owens almost didn't make it to Berlin because the United States had considered boycotting the Olympics over Hitler's treatment of Jews, but many African Americans opposed a boycott, yearning to prove their ability on a level playing field. Owens emerged as the biggest star of the Olympics, setting or equaling records in the 100-meter dash, the 200-meter sprint, the 400-meter relay, and the long jump. German crowds enthusiastically applauded his performances, deepening Hitler's humiliation.

Owens returned home to the oppression of Jim Crow, pointing out that while he didn't shake hands with Hitler, he wasn't invited to shake hands with the American president either. Lacking a college degree, forced through back doors and to the backs of buses, Owens subsisted on low-paying jobs such as pumping gas and demeaning public appearances such as racing against horses.

Still, Owens's victories not only shattered the myth of white athletic superiority but also established a black man as a hero for America and one of the greatest athletes of all time.

32

Gordon Parks

PHOTOGRAPHER, DIRECTOR • 1912–2006

Born in Fort Scott, Kansas, Gordon Parks bought his first camera at a pawnshop and taught himself how to use it. He made a name for himself while working at the Farm Security Administration, a government agency that was fighting rural poverty. He went on to become the first African American photographer on the staff of *Life* magazine and produced some of the best photo essays the world has ever seen, from showing what it meant to be black in America to telling the story of a twelve-year-old in the slums of Rio de Janeiro. He said that the camera was his weapon against racism and poverty.

Parks's work for *Vogue* in the 1950s changed the expectations of what an African American photographer could be doing. He went to Paris, Cuba, and the streets of New York City, creating pictures that showed the world of high fashion that few people of color had been able to reach.

Parks was the first African American director of major motion pictures, starting with *The Learning Tree* in 1969 and *Shaft* in 1971. These movies helped to increase the number of jobs for African Americans in films, from actors in front of the camera to producers and directors behind it. Parks wrote nearly two dozen books on subjects ranging from poetry to photography.

Parks's work transformed how later generations of black artists, photographers, and musicians saw themselves and the world, opening their imaginations to storytelling through pictures of the black experience.

Because he brought us pictures of black America

Because he ushered in the modern black leading man

33

Sidney Poitier

ACTOR, FILMMAKER • 1927–

In 1964, Sidney Poitier became the first African American to win an Academy Award for a leading role. In *Lilies of the Field,* he played a handyman who encounters a group of German, Austrian, and Hungarian nuns who believe that he's been heaven-sent. Some may say the same about Poitier's career. Poitier challenged Americans to change their idea about what a movie star looked like.

He starred in three important films in 1967 that centered on race and race relations. In *To Sir, with Love,* he was a teacher dealing with racial and social issues at a school in London. *In the Heat of the Night* introduced a black detective who was investigating a murder in a small southern town. And *Guess Who's Coming to Dinner* addressed interracial relationships in the same year that the Supreme Court overturned a Virginia law that prohibited blacks and whites from marrying each other.

Although he was born in Miami, Poitier grew up in his parents' native Bahamas. After a brief stint with the U.S. Army during World War II, he joined the influential American Negro Theater in Harlem and soon afterward started to appear in movies.

Poitier understood the importance of having someone who looked like him step behind the camera, too. He directed several important movies for black folks, including *Uptown Saturday Night* and *Let's Do It Again* (both of which he also starred in) and the comedy *Stir Crazy,* which featured the ebony-and-ivory pairing of Richard Pryor and Gene Wilder. Among his many honors, Poitier was awarded the Presidential Medal of Freedom by Barack Obama.

34

Richard Pryor

COMEDIAN • 1940–2005

Richard Pryor had a tough time growing up, including being abandoned by his mother. Searching for relief, he would often go to the movies. Little did he know that years later he would be appearing in them.

After a stint in the Army, Pryor started singing in small clubs near his home in Peoria, Illinois. But he soon discovered that people would rather hear him tell jokes. He began performing in comedy clubs, and before too long, he was doing appearances on some of the biggest television shows of the time.

Despite his success, he began to feel that his act wasn't authentic, and he changed it in a way that influenced every comedian that came after him. Pryor started to tell humorous, but honest, stories about himself and the poor and struggling people he knew from his childhood. He cursed a lot, just like real people do. And he wasn't afraid to make fun of white people.

His comedy was full of the truth that black folks usually said in private. Pryor would talk about his problems with drugs and relationships. Later, when he suffered from multiple sclerosis, he would joke about that, too. His comedy was rooted in pain, but audiences recognized the truth in it.

Pryor starred in two of his own television shows and a number of movies, including several comedies. Over the course of his career, he won an Emmy, five Grammys, and the first Mark Twain Prize for American Humor from the Kennedy Center, perhaps the biggest honor for a career in comedy.

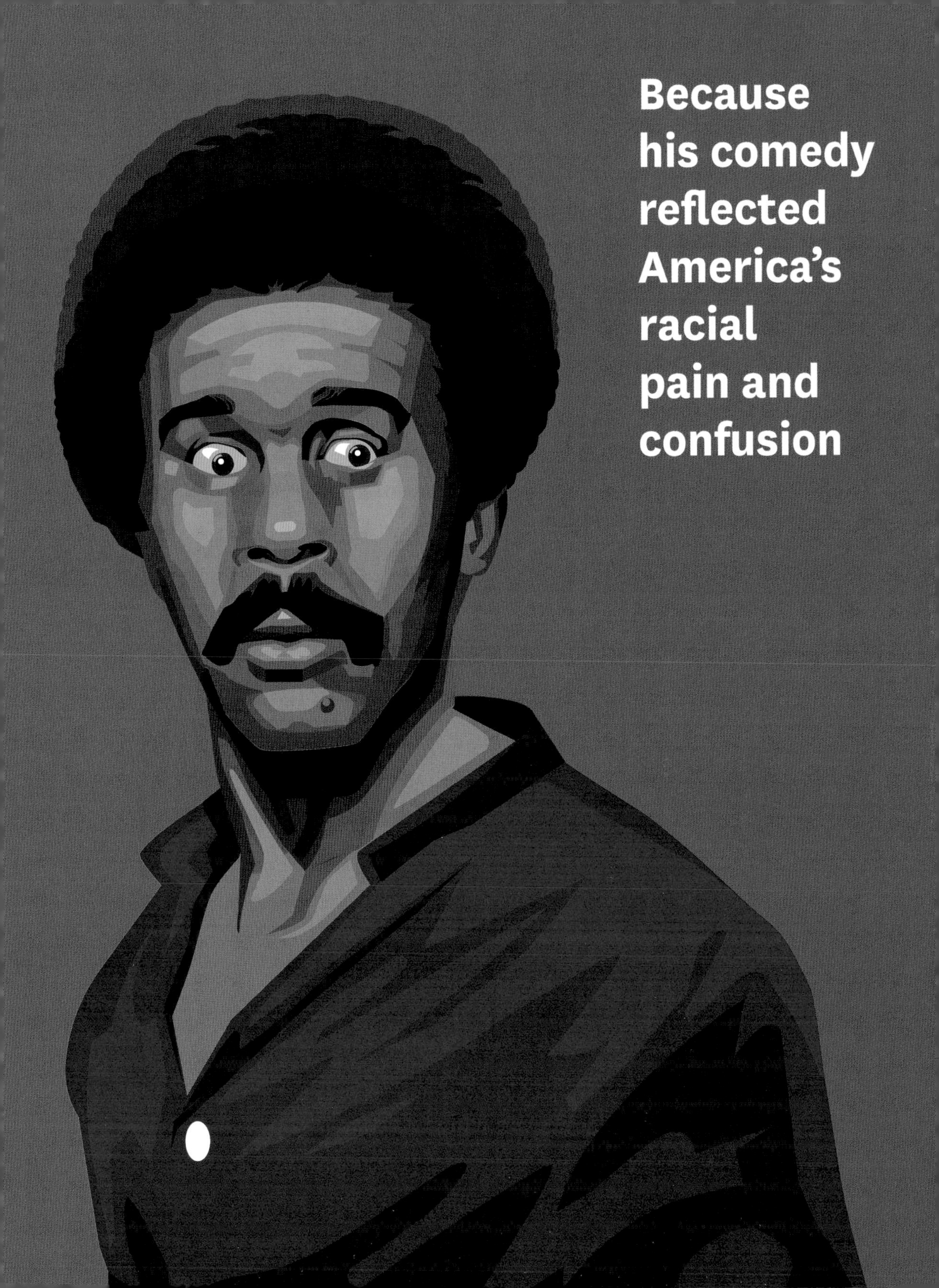
Because his comedy reflected America's racial pain and confusion

Because he was
the man who
knocked
Jim
Crow
out of
the park

35

Jackie Robinson

BASEBALL PLAYER, CIVIL RIGHTS ACTIVIST • 1919–72

On April 15, 1947, Jackie Robinson played first base for the Brooklyn Dodgers in a home game against the Boston Braves. He was the first African American to take the field in the big leagues in the modern era, and that day not only changed baseball but helped change the country, too.

Robinson was a terrific player. That first year, he led the league in stolen bases and won the inaugural Rookie of the Year Award. In his ten years in the major leagues, he was named to six All-Star teams and led Brooklyn to its only World Series title in 1955.

But he was an even more remarkable man. Baseball was the most important sport in America at the time, and Robinson was chosen to integrate the game because he could handle virulent racism from white players and white fans without losing his temper.

Indeed, the best way to think about the importance of Robinson is to consider what would have happened if he had failed. Segregation was the law across the South. In the North, a system of economic and cultural repression kept the races apart. If Robinson had quit or retaliated against all the hateful names and slights, his opponents would have used him as proof that African Americans were incapable of joining white society.

Robinson's success created a path for African American achievements in other industries—baseball integrated even before the military. After he left baseball, Robinson continued to work hard for black empowerment, writing for newspapers and challenging presidents to advance the cause of civil rights.

Robinson's courage and achievement at a time when Jim Crow laws deprived black citizens of basic human rights marked an important turning point in black history.

36

Sojourner Truth

ABOLITIONIST, ACTIVIST • 1797–1883

Sojourner Truth is most famous for words she may never have spoken.

A traveling preacher who advocated for women's rights and abolition, Truth gave a speech at the Women's Rights Convention in Akron, Ohio, in 1851 calling for equal treatment for black women:

"That man over there says that women need to be helped into carriages, and lifted over ditches, and to have the best place everywhere. Nobody ever helps me into carriages, or over mud-puddles, or gives me any best place! And ain't I a woman?" The message was powerful, but it's unlikely the words are exact. They come from a version published years after the event using a stereotypical Southern dialect. Truth, however, grew up in New York, and Dutch was her first language.

Regardless, Truth was famous. Her memoir, *The Narrative of Sojourner Truth: A Northern Slave,* was published in 1850, and she toured and spoke before large crowds. She was the ninth child in an enslaved family and escaped as an adult with her own infant daughter. Born Isabella Baumfree, she gave herself the name "Sojourner Truth" after becoming a Methodist. During the Civil War, she helped recruit black troops for the Union Army, which granted her the opportunity to speak with President Abraham Lincoln.

Truth died in 1883 at her home in Battle Creek, Michigan. Four decades later, the constitutional amendment extending the vote to women was ratified.

Because
of a
famous
speech
amid a
lifetime of
activism

Because she was a
conductor on the
Underground
Railroad

Harriet Tubman

ABOLITIONIST • 1820–1913

Harriet Tubman was born into slavery and endured physical violence nearly every day in her early years. In one incident, Tubman encountered a slave who had left the fields without permission. When she refused to restrain the runaway, an overseer hurled a two-pound weight at Tubman, striking her in the head. The attack left her with headaches and seizures for the rest of her life.

Tubman escaped from slavery in 1849 using the Underground Railroad, a secret network of antislavery activists and safe houses, to make the ninety-mile trip from her home in Maryland to Philadelphia. But her own safety wasn't enough. Hearing that her niece and her niece's children were going to be sold, Tubman went back and led them to Philadelphia. Soon she returned for her siblings. Then for her parents.

After passage of the 1850 Fugitive Slave Act, which required that slaves who escaped to the North be seized and returned to slavery, Tubman changed her route so it ended in Canada, where slavery was outlawed. Even though there was a bounty for her capture, she made at least nineteen trips and led hundreds of people to freedom.

During the Civil War, Tubman became a nurse and spy for the Union government. She tended to the sick and wounded, caring for soldiers both black and white. After the war, Tubman was active in the women's suffrage movement and is now considered an American icon.

38

Madam C. J. Walker

ENTREPRENEUR, ACTIVIST • 1867–1919

Sarah Breedlove, the poor washerwoman who would become millionaire entrepreneur Madam C. J. Walker, was trying to cure dandruff and banish her bald spots when she mixed her first batch of petrolatum and medicinal sulfur.

But what began as a solution to a pesky personal problem quickly became a means to a greater end. With the sale of each two-ounce tin of Madam C. J. Walker's Wonderful Hair Grower, she discovered that her most powerful gift was motivating other women. As she traveled throughout the United States, the Caribbean, and Central America, teaching her Walker System and training sales agents, she shared her personal story: her birth on the same plantation where her parents had been enslaved, her struggles as a young widow, her desperate poverty. If she could transform herself, so could they. In place of washtubs and cotton fields, Walker offered women beauty, education, financial freedom, and confidence.

The more money Walker made, the more generous she became, donating to her local black YMCA in Indianapolis and the NAACP's antilynching fund, establishing college scholarships, and paying for lessons for young black musicians. In 1917, at the first national convention for her company, Walker awarded prizes to the women who sold the most products or recruited the most new agents. More important, Walker honored the delegates whose local clubs had contributed the most to charity.

Walker urged President Woodrow Wilson to support legislation that would make lynching a federal crime. She was labeled a "Negro subversive" by the War Department because of her advocacy for black soldiers during World War I.

A pioneer of today's multibillion-dollar hair care industry, Walker defied stereotypes, provided employment for thousands of women, and donated large sums to civic, educational, and political causes. And all of it started with hair ointment.

Because she leveraged
black beauty to
become a
self-made
millionaire

Because he
brought education
to the South

39

Booker T. Washington

EDUCATOR, CIVIL RIGHTS ACTIVIST • 1856–1915

Not long after the end of the Civil War, Booker T. Washington, who had been born into slavery, started Tuskegee Institute in 1881 with thirty students, two thousand dollars, and a one-room shack. Southern whites saw an educated Negro as dangerous, so Washington told them that his students did not want equal rights. Instead, he said, they wanted to learn trades such as carpentry and printing and contribute to Southern prosperity. Donations from Northern whites poured in, and Tuskegee was allowed to grow.

In 1895, Washington was the only black speaker to address a mostly white audience at an important meeting in Atlanta called the Cotton States and International Exposition. In his speech, which critics later called the "Atlanta Compromise," Washington advised black men and women to work with their hands, stay in the South, and accept white supremacy in exchange for economic security.

That speech helped make Washington the most influential black person in America at the time. He became an advisor to both President William McKinley and President Theodore Roosevelt on racial matters. Washington lectured around the country, helped start the National Negro Business League, and published a best-selling autobiography. While black intellectuals such as W. E. B. Du Bois chafed at the way he seemed to defer to whites, Washington used his influence to place African Americans in jobs across the country and secretly fund challenges to Jim Crow laws. When Washington died in 1915, the campus where he is buried had grown to fifteen hundred students and one hundred buildings, with a two-million-dollar endowment.

40

Ida B. Wells

JOURNALIST, CIVIL RIGHTS ACTIVIST • 1862–1931

Ida B. Wells was a superhero of journalism. After three of her friends were murdered by a mob in Memphis, Tennessee, in 1892, she started to investigate the widespread horror of lynching. Wells faced down threats of death and torture for bringing international attention and shame to the whites who terrorized black communities in the United States after Reconstruction.

Just as many people could not believe the atrocities committed in World War II concentration camps, Wells encountered widespread denial and disbelief as she wrote about the barbaric acts of her countrymen in the pages of the *Memphis Free Speech,* the newspaper she co-owned.

Documenting the epidemic of lynching was miserable, disheartening work. But Wells also found time to advocate for voting rights and civil rights of black women like herself. She wasn't much concerned with being polite about it, either. For her troubles, she was criticized for being unladylike and dirty-minded.

Yet Wells represented the best of American journalism. She dared America to confront its hypocrisies and live up to the ideals upon which the country was founded. Wells's crusade lives on today in those who document the killing of unarmed black people by police. She lives on in black women who not only exercise their right to vote but also, like her, run for office. (Wells ran for a seat in the Illinois State Senate.) She lives on in the words and deeds of the NAACP, which she cofounded. No wonder Wells was known by the subtitle of her best-known biography: *A Sword Among Lions.*

Because she
made the world
see what was
happening
to black
America

Because she's
simply the
best

41

Serena Williams

TENNIS PLAYER • 1981–

In any conversation about the greatest athletes, one name rises to the top—Serena Williams.

She has enough victories for several lifetimes. She's won more Grand Slam singles titles than any other woman in the modern era. She's also won four Olympic gold medals, fourteen Grand Slam doubles titles, and a Career Golden Slam (singles titles from each of the sport's four major events plus an Olympic gold medal in singles).

Williams is the youngest of five daughters. Her father, a former sharecropper from Louisiana, learned from books and videos how to coach Serena and her older sister Venus. The Williams sisters had daily two-hour practices on a concrete court, avoiding potholes and often practicing without nets. Growing up in Compton, California, meant being a fighter and developing a tough skin—which would characterize their game on and off the court.

Williams transcended tennis, a historically white sport, by being herself—with incredible strength, dedication, and an energetic style of play. What makes Williams's career so remarkable is her spirit to rise above criticism of her appearance, game, and body and still be the best year after year.

Whether she's serving tennis balls, designing affordable fashion, or teaming up with Beyoncé in music videos, Williams's resumé solidifies her place among sports' all-time greats.

42

August Wilson

PLAYWRIGHT • 1945–2005

Playwright August Wilson made it his life's work to document, explain, and validate the everyday lives of African Americans.

Between 1984, when *Ma Rainey's Black Bottom* premiered, and 2005, when he died at age sixty, Wilson produced what he called the American Century Cycle. It consisted of one play for every decade of the twentieth century, a trajectory that went from the aftermath of slavery through the Great Migration and the civil rights movement to the dawn of gentrification.

Wilson's body of work stands as one of the greatest in the history of dramatic literature. He won two Pulitzer Prizes and multiple Tony and New York Drama Critics' Circle Awards.

Raised in Pittsburgh, Wilson set nearly all his work in his home neighborhood of the Hill District. Yet it was only when he moved to largely white St. Paul, Minnesota, in his thirties that he began to fully hear and channel the spoken-word poetry of the musicians, preachers, gamblers, jitney drivers, and sanitation workers among whom he had lived.

With the American Century Cycle, Wilson transmuted their voices into art for the ages.

Because he is America's Shakespeare

Because
she turned a
talk show into
a self-help
movement

43

Oprah Winfrey

MEDIA MOGUL, PHILANTHROPIST • 1954–

When *The Oprah Winfrey Show* started broadcasting nationally in 1986, it turned television, especially the daytime talk show, into something new. For starters, had she gotten into the television business only ten years earlier, the Mississippi-born Winfrey wouldn't have been let anywhere near the set: she wasn't white, blond, thin, or male.

Winfrey's superhero talent was getting people to really like her and relate to her. The way she confessed her own weaknesses made self-help feel modern and chic. And she didn't inspire just black people. Women of all races eagerly joined her movement to "Live Your Best Life," which was the title of one of her books.

Winfrey used her position as host of one of the longest-running daytime talk shows in television history to become a multimedia phenomenon. She's the owner of a cable TV network. She's a movie actress and a Broadway musical producer. She started a book club that made instant bestsellers. She's helped launch the careers of numerous television hosts and self-help gurus, including Dr. Phil, Iyanla Vanzant, Dr. Oz, Suze Orman, Nate Berkus, Rachael Ray, Bob Greene, and Gayle King. Since the debut of *O, The Oprah Magazine* in April 2000, she's been on the cover of every issue, making her one of the most influential cover models in magazine publishing history. Her early endorsement of Barack Obama helped him win the Democratic Party nomination for president. She is the first African American female billionaire.

Her generosity, especially for educational endeavors, is legendary. Winfrey funded a girls-only private school in South Africa and scholarships for hundreds of students at Morehouse College. In 2011, she won an Academy Award for her international humanitarian efforts.

44

Stevie Wonder

SINGER-SONGWRITER, PRODUCER • 1950–

Since 1961, when the blind eleven-year-old musical prodigy auditioned for Motown Records, Stevie Wonder has composed a full catalog of songs about love, compassion, justice, and unity. And his music still fills dance floors today.

Born Stevland Judkins, he was given the name "Stevie Wonder" by Motown founder Berry Gordy. Wonder's first number one hit came in 1963 when he was only thirteen with "Fingertips, Part 2," which referred to the song's bongo rhythms. In 2016, he released "Faith" with Ariana Grande. In between came dozens and dozens of timeless songs, melodies, and moments.

No other musician has pulled so many heartstrings with a harmonica while simultaneously jamming so ferociously on the piano. Wonder wrote, produced, and played multiple instruments on the Spinners' 1970 hit "It's a Shame" and created his own hits, such as "Signed, Sealed, Delivered I'm Yours," "Superstition," "Living for the City," and "Sir Duke."

All along, he has maintained an unrelenting social consciousness. Some stars flitted in and out of the struggle, but Wonder remained, writing about the problems facing those on the bottom, like his song "You Haven't Done Nothin'," a stinging rebuke of President Richard Nixon. His 1966 cover of Bob Dylan's "Blowin' in the Wind" became an anthem of the civil rights movement. And his version of "Happy Birthday" helped persuade America to accept a holiday honoring Martin Luther King Jr.

And always, with Wonder, black love was nurturing and empowering, a continuous source of validation and strength. Half a century later, in an era when most black music superstars dwell on earthly obsessions, Wonder continues to elevate us to higher ground.

Because
nobody has
uplifted
more spirits

Acknowledgments

We are grateful to many colleagues at ESPN, the parent company of The Undefeated, for their help and support of this book. They include President James Pitaro, Executive Vice President Connor Schell, Senior Vice President Robert King, Vice Presidents Julie Sobieski and Daniel Sassoon, Assistant Chief Counsel Peter Scher, and Senior Creative Director Chin Wang.

Big props to The Undefeated writers who helped craft the profiles: Bruce Britt, Howard Bryant, A'Lelia Bundles, Danielle Cadet, Kelley L. Carter, David Dennis Jr., Aaron Dodson, Kelley D. Evans, Michael A. Fletcher, Samuel G. Freedman, Jill Hudson, Derrick Z. Jackson, Martenzie Johnson, Maya A. Jones, Trudy Joseph, Raina Kelley, Brent Lewis, Callan Mathis, Soraya Nadia McDonald, Kevin Merida, John X. Miller, Lonnae O'Neal, April Reign, Brando Simeo Starkey, Justin Tinsley, and Jesse Washington.

And many thanks to those who were instrumental in putting together the original online version of *The Fierce 44* or who otherwise helped to bring this book to completion: Karin Berry, Sabrina Clarke, Kate Elazegui, Breana Jones, Justin McCraw, Ashley Melfi, Paul Schreiber, Beth Stojkov, and Khari Williams.